Kimberly Reyes insists that we remember the h[...]
erased by the work of empire and patriarchy. Tr[...]
and historical eras, Reyes utilizes archive, video [...], [...], [...]
unrelenting lens that refuses "a cozy invisibility." This collection affirms the
need to preserve histories on the precipice of being consumed and forgotten.
Through the visual use of gradient text, Reyes amplifies and conjures what
is at risk of being sent into the silence of white noise. Be it in California,
Ireland, Puerto Rico, or popular culture, Reyes calls our attention to the
"ivory-stroked / false purity—" and the "misappropriation // of American
gothic / how blackness sits / unbound // darkest places unimaged." Amid
all the weight, there is a tender cradling of the lyric that re-animates a sense
of home and a refusal to be displaced: "we are still / we are memory."
vanishing point. is rich in language and it is a gift to follow Reyes as she
delves into what must be known and what must be spoken to sculpt and
imagine a new cartography.
—Anthony Cody, author of *Borderland Apocrypha*

Kimberly Reyes has written an innovative and magnetic book. Each
poem spirals beautifully by itself but when I finished reading, I realized I
had encountered and entered new architecture. Here, thinking radiates to
illuminate the 'absorbing ghosts' of the self and the familial and the 'living
shadows' of oppressive historical forces. Here, the language is lyrical,
layered, and spectral. Here, the 'hyphen is a rejection of negative space.'
Reyes is an astonishingly gifted poet and this book enlarges and complicates
what the page can hold back, reveal.
—Eduardo C. Corral, author of *Guillotine*

Kimberly Reyes' latest collection *vanishing point.* contains hauntings
within the text, echoes in the graphics. There are diagrams and QR codes,
landscape and demographics that impress upon readers the emptiness from
missing—that map of dispossessions, the collapse of stars—and the fullness
of looking, of looking closer. Here, people faced with survival keep looking
back and up and through disaster to ask: Who are the living? or: What does
it feel like? and: Is this pleasure? This is a thoughtful, serious exploration of
expirations and hollows, stains and swells, the soil salted over blood, flame,
memory.
—Ladan Osman, author of *Exiles of Eden*

vanishing point. ranges effortlessly over epochs, oceans, continents, casting a wryly compassionate, implacable eye on North America, Southern Ireland and the complex histories that bind them. It consolidates one of the freshest, most searching voices on either side of the Atlantic
—Billy Ramsell, author of *The Architect's Dream of Winter*

vanishing point. suggests a disappearance, and the print does occasionally fade from black to gray, yet the poems in this book present a vivid original presence by means of adroit language, strong emotion, imaginative leaps. It is a unique work, wide-ranging, heart-rending—attuned to the multiple forms of who one is, black and certainly blue. But also multiple and nuanced in the twists and turns of lines, sound, spacing, vocabulary—a complexity that can't help but rattle and move the reader. The poems are wonderfully attentive to rhythm, even as they include QR codes, documents, quotations, and the words of others, for example, Fred Moten, Kara Walker, Richard Wright, Sinéad O'Connor, those echoed words in gray.

VP raises the significant questions of where one belongs and who one is, but it is also a book of tenderness and compassion for the larger world where destruction exists in history, around every corner, for those who pick grapes, for black women, for race horses, for birds ("for every bird there is a stone/ thrown at a bird…for every child/there is a womb cold.")

No one with roots doubled under
Can survive these days
I tried I've travelled I'm tired
Quickly decipher—lyrebird, starling
Define invasive species
Can't tell if it's a crow or my stomach
God protect me from its sensual coo

—Martha Ronk, author of *The Place One Is*

Previously Published Poetry

Running to Stand Still, Omnidawn Publishing, 2019.

Warning Coloration, dancing girl press, 2018.

vanishing point.

Cover art by Harry Clarke

Cover design by Shanna Compton
Interior design by Kimberly Reyes and Laura Joakimson
Interior typeface: Times New Roman

Library of Congress Cataloging-in-Publication Data

Names: Reyes, Kimberly, 1977- author.
Title: vanishing point. / Kimberly Reyes.

Description: Oakland, California : Omnidawn Publishing, 2023. | Summary:
"Kimberly Reyes navigates the physical, hereditary, and liminal worlds
between land, time, and memory. Reclaiming and examining space in San
Francisco, Ireland, and the Atlantic Ocean, the author performs séance
and autopsy of all we see and do not see, and all we have left behind"--
Provided by publisher.

Identifiers: LCCN 2022057663 | ISBN 9781632431196 (trade paperback)
Classification: LCC PS3618.E9386 V36 2023 | DDC 811/.6--dc23/eng/20221205
LC record available at https://lccn.loc.gov/202205766

Published by Omnidawn Publishing, Oakland, California
www.omnidawn.com
10 9 8 7 6 5 4 3 2 1
ISBN: 978-1-63243-119-6

vanishing point.

Kimberly Reyes

OMNIDAWN PUBLISHING
OAKLAND CALIFORNIA
2023

Contents

Preamble

You must not try to be too pure, you must fly closer to the sea.

—Sinéad O'Connor
I Do Not Want What I Haven't Got

Sonnets

The Poet Extrapolates & Animates Frederick Douglass's Life-Changing Journey to the UK & Ireland in a Semi-Formal Sonnet (or what I think *well-meaning* white folks want to hear) **as Part I**

The Poet Then Interpolates Her First Journey Across the Atlantic (what I think I mean to say) **in a Contemporary Sonnet as Part II.**

Frederick Douglass
Victoria Hotel, Belfast,
January 1, 1846

To William Lloyd Garrison

I can truly say, I have spent some of the happiest moments of my life since landing in this country.

I seem to have undergone a transformation.

I live a new life... Eleven days and a half gone, and I have crossed three thousand miles of the perilous deep. Instead of a democratic government, I am under a monarchical government.

Instead of the bright blue sky of America, I am covered with the soft grey fog of the Emerald Isle.

I breathe, and lo! the chattel becomes a man.

I gaze around in vain for one who will question my equal humanity,

claim me as his slave, or offer me an insult.

I employ a cab—I am seated

beside white people—

I reach the hotel—I enter the same door—I am shown into the same parlor—I dine at the same table—and no one is offended. No delicate nose grows deformed in my presence.

I find no difficulty here in obtaining admission into any place of worship, instruction or amusement, on equal terms with people

as white as any

I ever saw in the United States.

I meet nothing to remind me of my complexion. I find myself regarded and treated at every turn with the kindness and deference paid to white people.[1]

Part I

I don't know at what port he stood, which oars

he stalled, inhaling mist & saline film

a splicing to a Point of No Return,

for lucidity   shuffling about decks.

What's stolen for Van Diemen's Land, Charleston?

What of asylum granted, hope harbored

with   abandon?   A branded pastel gale,

calcified boats, still frames in / Cobh / Cape Coast

familial fetters boring tide, gall,   bloat

16

there is resolution in this water

Yemayá sang,   ports rang (!) calls from Dublin,

Cork, Liverpool,   a confluence of time

at the River Mersey.   Grave blue & white

waters carried their son, born to anchor.

Part II

I know what it's like to stand facing Celtic ice, saltwater racing past skin burning under a muted sun, a Holyhead[2] haze. I remember thinking that quiver was a baptizing in all my ancestry.

I was sixteen that first time I took a ferry to Ireland. A Spring Break trip with my white classmates my parents couldn't really afford, which made that phone call to my mom from the North London hotel, the day before leaving England, so much worse. Through gasps & dried salt I cry-whispered back to Queens about two men who suspended lunch, screaming in spit & Scottish accents about *silverware* (!), the restaurant had to *discard the knives & forks* because *a monkey*--I *had eaten* there.

When the ferry docked we walked past locals, some Travelers, eager for strangers, fresh squeak & coin. A blonde child, face covered in soot (just the way Frank McCourt described!), eyes wide & eager-blue screamed with her heart & pointer finger: "Blackie!" My classmates cowered, I laughed, exhausted by what we didn't yet know of land, ladders, & scales.

Twenty years later I would read about Frederick Douglass, perhaps the greatest American, & how he felt 'seen' as a man for the first time in a room full of white people. His recognition of this is still celebrated (!). As if being defined in a crowd or the glare of whiteness isn't an unending proposition.

---

[1]Frederick Douglass, [Letter], Victoria Hotel, Belfast, January 1, 1846. To William Lloyd Garrison. Foner, Philip (ed). Life and Writings of Frederick Douglass. New York: International Publishers, 1950. Vol. I, p. 125. // Garrison, Douglass's 'white ally' & benefactor of sorts, **used** this letter in his newspaper, The Liberator.

[2]Holyhead is a port in Wales that connects the UK to Ireland // Leaving England, one must tread over a *sovereignish* state of The United Kingdom of Great Britain to get to The Republic of Ireland.

We are all drowned out

If you respect the dead
and recall where they died

In 1711 New York, nearly 1,000
out of about 6,400 New Yorkers
were Black, and at least 40 percent
of the white households
included a slave.*

by this time tomorrow
there will be nowhere to walk.
—Katie Ford

Tracing in journey from
grandmother's grave—

terrified
rime reforests.

Branched-claws
scrape

       thin hours—eleven on I-95
       careening coast.

     Ivory-stroked asphalt
doppler-shift's the course

   rearview cemeteries,
   rank exhaust,

salt-fog mired,
Green Book-guided,

memorial over tire—
our open books of harbor.

South Carolina is still
hailing

scourged babies
who are the living

                    Five Points

                                        290 Broadway

            Seneca Falls

New York
second to Charleston:

auctions,
wet markets,

an infestation,
diseased greed,

            stunted seedlings,
            crown weeds

                    collect
            witching hour dew.

I sideswipe back—
            ports of call &

sub   surface
cargo |

                        Here** there's a crying
                        blue child in Cobh

I can only
hear near the sea.

*Columbia University's MAAP (Mapping the African American Past)
**Cobh, County Cork was Ireland's largest port of departure for emigration to America
(and to penal colonies in Australia, as U2's "Van Diemen's Land" memorializes). It was
also the last stopping point of the Titanic, as well as the port of call for many doomed
military vessels. A hotel built in 1854, formerly known as the Queen's Hotel, served as a
morgue & makeshift hospital for nautical & wartime fatalities. The structure is rumored
to be a soul cage for drowned victims of all ages, including the ghost of a "blue" child
said to be heard screaming on its upper floors.

Part I
The Coasts

Paradise as tinder

Soon at least 86 people would be dead in a new and ferocious kind of climate change-inflected wildfire. And Paradise would suffer a fate that appears increasingly likely: the total destruction of a modern American city.
—*The Guardian*

The lined white stalks
of the Silverado trail
aren't graves
as much as flyers:

the fire sale
in Paradise.

Crimson-black grapes
hang taut before
the harvesting
flame, coughing

       celestial particles
       of one another—
       caked windshields,
       ashed arm hair—

       we could be carrying
       persons, deer,
       inhaling fear

       all the way down
       in San Francisco

          a milieu of haze,
          indifference.

                (At least 86 cindered
                hands
                some used to cast the vote

for the 45th,
pull the lever
from the root,
their own
prescribed fires

that's their story

about how to squelch,
about how wine is
made on plantations,
about how red & ripe
farm country is,
has always been,
especially on coastal
plains.)

Here's what's true:

Winemaking is a cruel horticulture.

You must sanitize the grapes, their
sediment, first removing the stem

(the remains to ferment, foreign neglect,
chambered cool;
preserving a whiteness
is avoiding any touch of skin)

a palate cleanse.

Then the stomping,

conversion, abashing
on pillaged land,
a new sick,

a bleeding
through a royal blue
& bone-white
linen.

Can you taste it?

This land is ripe
the land is bitter
the land needs to burn

as we
anesthetize time
& tinder
bottling up consequence.

The Great Race Place

Ancient horses roamed the North American continent for millions of years. And many, many years later, horses played an integral role in building the foundation of the United States. However, there was a period in time when horses vanished from the continent, and the reason remains unknown...

Santa Anita's
crushing bets,
cracking backs—
bone underfoot

blank fire—kickback—panic

...while horses in North America vanished, those that had migrated out of the continent survived and thrived. ...

our wildness
clutches the race card.

After hoof,
soot, utility
has caked
into a brown "U"

a bulb dims over the pedigreed
in the waste plant

an unassuming man
avoiding razed eyes

skins the bodies.

                                        In the corner
                                        a sold mare furrows

                                        —pain killer &
                                        a shot of memory—

                                        tracks of tripwire
                                        congeal screams
                                        lacing her ponytail.

What does our man bring home?

*... In the late 1400s, Spanish conquistadors brought European horses to North
America, back to where they evolved long ago.*

Does he commandeer blinders?

He might read about knights
who coddle their loyal horses
while brushing his
daughters' manes.

He might end the night
kissing his oldest,
his namesake,
over their shared crimson
curls, while she lifts her
freckled hands
in prayer.

---

pbs.org

We're Going to Save Us

God put me on Earth to do what I did. He made me.
—Samuel Little

                    we are our unborn, we are

                    we

                    are directing   us
                                                    out
                    it's our emergency
                                              ours
                                                        only

            our   only
                     /
                 exit

His
a small calling,

he silenced by spurning
bond & coil

we hear it though
subaltern

 echo
 /   \

a yelping   of dogs   men   flame
bulging   shame   prayer & blows
                                  | a cruel unison of
                                  churches &
                                  shrapnel   scalped
                                  braids & bows |

a wild crimson mud   lash bracing—
the warm swollen   release

when a man unbuckles

we are wet
we are still —

African-American, Native American and Alaska Native women die of
pregnancy-related causes at a rate about three times higher than those of white
women.
—*The New York Times*

we are still

we are memory
silent chorus
we are still.

We are still
            \\

                in unborn community
                our unfertilized
                saw the eyes of famine
                fled Guineamen
                fell from ships

                felled custody.

                They now wade
                & warn about

                execution.

                Our DNA know
                scale, land

                & terror
                their free gulls
                did not breach.

Samuel Little's FBI sketches via FBI.com

Séance at the Beauty Parlor

...she stopped using relaxers two decades ago after talking to a
client who performed autopsies:
'How they identified black women a lot of times was a green layer
                        on top of the brain from relaxing '*
                                —WSB-TV Atlanta
Under poaching pressure, elephants are evolving to lose their
tusks—National Geographic

We will us away we cannot stay **we worn** our crowns our crowns
we will us away **we incarnate** our crowns our crowns our crowns

we cannot **we eradicate** our crowns our crowns our crowns we we

we weary / we in our crowns our crowns our crowns our crowns we
cannot say **we** or our crowns our crowns our crowns our crowns we
will us away we **warn** / **we absorb** our crowns our crowns our crows

What

                                                object lye
                                n' bone

torching
                        long memory

                        helical
                                pastures

We will us away we cannot stay **we mourn** our crowns our crows
we will us away **we incinerate** our crowns our crowns our crown

our will to **celebrate** our crowns our crowns our crowns our crow

37

we wear / we / our crowns our crowns our crowns our crowns we
cannot stay we our crowns our crowns our crowns our crowns we
will us away we cannot afford our crowns our crowns our crowns

    meanwhile elephants

    forage
                   coiling
                 war:
            prize & bullseye
        evolving
                     whole hollow

'n. tusk we cannot lose our crowns the crow in crowns our crowns

we cannot stay our crowns our crowns our crowns our crowns we
will us away we form / contour our crowns our crowns our crown

foregoing curl   horns of scourge   skull   calloused halo

    *a chemical

    treatment

    to straighten

    curls

    collapsing

    hair shaft

    bonds

22 months.

As a child I went to the Central Park Zoo with my father. We followed a sign
that read: "This way to see the world's most dangerous animal!"
Something like that.
I only remember he was holding my hand.
When we arrived at the exhibit there was just a mirror.
—Poet

Elephants gestate
longer than any mammal.

More-fertile species
—seals, sea lions, rats &
wombats—find survival in time,

aka "embryonic diapause," a delayed
implantation — allowing fertilized eggs to
remain in a suspended state until conditions
are just right. A mother suspends the world
for better conditions,   motherhood ajourns
for favorable weather, an abundance of food;
or just until a more welcoming colony, herd,
mischief, or wisdom appears. Humans know
very little about this miracle beyond technical
terms. We think we know that elephants &
the world's most dangerous creature cannot
endure this duty, but both species can
mourn memories, & their reflections.

Ascension

The machines crush her
breasts quiet.

There is no cancer in the family,
she's arguing in an exacting box.

Really, now?
| Latino (not Black)|
|Black (not Hispanic)|

You're floating. Your trauma glows in the dark. Inside you blips &
irregularities. A cluster of malformed cells. A mass of stress. Lumps of
hard reality. Hate in cavities only radiologists see.

It escalates quickly.
Lying on her back
abstract consent.
Yes or no.
There's a glint inside her frame.
They need it out.

For the first time in years, momentum, sober tears—
a cotton pillow forcing frizz.

> No, you can't lose your hair. (!) Your grace. It's that
> 3C/4A good in you. Soft hiding space. You hope this
> isn't what the test reasons. You memorize stucco
> on the ceiling, keep from blinking. You identify a
> feeling.

She's soaking the pillow.
The doctor holds her hand.

You'll feel a bit of cold & wet.

The painkiller pierces her
slack skin / an addiction
to celled destruction.
What is low grade mania?
More than a hangover?

You feel relief rising, tingling, a needle for pilfering.
Upturned palms, engorged pores.
A pinch then pressure.

Is this pleasure?

Follow the tiles. An anesthetized waiting.

Swallow.

Who can store this with her?

Her mother, already disappointed
the news of antidepressants.

A past extracted.

A return to the "nerve pills"
her aunts / uncles
never stomached.

There is no escaping

family
history
boxes

Blink
Swallow
Blink

The softest part of you numb
you can't fear the beat.

The separation
—complete. *Hold the area.*

Place pressure.
This new hollow, over her heart.

**Rusty, this is a poem about
Lexapro**

A ripple of rime
tickling nape
      —traversing spine
spit-glazing raw awe.

Identify five elements ~~that~~ inhabit* your work.

~~Fire~~ *Cinder* - fuel & remnant.

~~Air~~, *Space* – the plasmatic, the conductor.

Time – a cruel confluence of the 1981 Culture Club song (of the same name), my need to answer rhetorical questions & Brittney Cooper's TED Talk on the racial politics (of it).

~~Water~~ *Currents* – echoes of misdirection.

~~Earth~~ *Roots* - clawing horizons.

*by cause, degree, circumstance, manner & place

Pirouettes

Whiskey-stained memories,
bronzed-brides atop
1970's wedding albums,

inside gated, rust-tolerant
shopping cart communities

tied to the edge of humanity,
the 8th marker, Ocean Beach.

Balmy saltwater beckons
blow ins, allies, we come as
scouring crows,

a reconnaissance,
our goodwill & imposition
draping ashen figures:

quiescent, ocean-
sprayed evictees nurturing
engorged cartons of milk.

We too play house,
toasting an expiration,
here here

raised glasses in the Dogpatch(!)—
a salutary spoiling
nonetheless.

On the ghettoization of childless women
After white feminism

I ride for the loudest tweeters, the Black birds,
us local girls holed up in barren districts
decent realtors renamed. Since all my babies
will have fur, I tell myself it's a mercy
to have never made family or home.
There's too much not here here to pass on.

For every flockless bird there is a stone
aimed at that bird & the pigeons here are
pretty aggressive. Scavenging is dangerous
& for every child & ring posted in sim
neighborhoods on socials,

(between your black boxes & brunch posts)

there are eggs frozen, leasing lab space. (For
the stragglers who've amassed fancy plumage,
anyway.)

Life is shorter & narrower than it should be for
those of us not meant for your social security
& amity is hard to come by, so I horde any
extra birdfeed in this pantry, for the

crows & ravens dumbing themselves down
for scraps

trapped in a cul-de-sac that's 40something%
terrifying.

The Fever Dream

The obsolete definition of
cope *is to encounter, to fight*
: to maintain a **contest**
or **combat** *usually on even*
terms or with success.
            It could also mean to
            cover *or furnish.*
—Merriam-Webster

A March of
nerve endings
            whispering
            skip tonight...

You want wine at your wedding
so *don't cross the line————*

May's a lash,
firm & familiar

            it's done
                    now,
            you become —

it's passed on & over.

August you'd start hiding
solutions,
nights clanking emptiness
on heavily soiled toes
you can see your own nose
on the way to recycling

barefoot
disassociated, far

from fooling
your agency,

& why
it takes a liter of spirits
for buoyancy.

What does it feel like?

your therapist asks

reward
for running with
every empty fist.

What does it feel like?

your favorite therapist

asks:

is this your longest relationship?

can you leave go
your most reliable escort?

will you unclench the hand?
that ties the other behind your back

How does it feel

bartering hollows?

What does it feel like?

folding into a
furnace

igniting a barren home.

Stain in creases

The whole answer is there on the canvas.
—Edward Hopper

Beyond the
gallery, our history
resonates:

Walker & Weems,
interned wings,
loud, counter migrations —
that exist in   & outside
of arm-crossed
South Carolina mournings —

to which I then need,
prefer, the art of echo

that may be realism (?)
a cozy invisibility

        picture me bussing
        in "Chop Suey"

        would I have been
        in the kitchen, at Phillies?

        in the pantry storing
        watching, growing

        the *darker sister…*
        I, too, am America

        an ars Americana
        etching of desolation

I can never put into
a proper word…

& I don't know
but need to think

he'd see straight through
me, if we ever didn't meet.

Tim Burton says I'm not his aesthetic

which I expected.

I know the misappropriation
of *American* gothic

how Blackness seeds
the bayou

humidity
of unburied fruit,

rice in the Carolinas
white-rife with grief.

I also know better—perhaps,
what it is to hold a man's knives,

have the ancestors scare away the vampires
reclaiming land over Calypso tunes,

Keaton's zebra snake Hoodoo.
& I know you like me
                          dancing,
impaling
grief—

Which is why, maybe, I even once almost
dated a white man before he *empathized* with me,

a Black woman,
said he'd once been fat,

**a bridge
to blackness (!),**

felt the stares,
his flesh aflame.

Perhaps he'd heard
the hooves of his

heedless horseman
hunting a Pecola Breedlove

aged in paling baggage—
her smeared red lip

Robert Smith has mimicked.
We're taught

the ocean's depth is
inconceivable, also

imagine needing
that feast

craving
our cornfed blood.

Part II
The Atlantic

A hyphen is a rejection of negative space
After Kara Walker

All I am, the African

the we

began
——-

                    trauma chains to mulch,
                    wood, port, salt, rice, rind,
                    far-off molasses pitches bind
                    white seas **American** mutation

& perhaps not entirely
perhaps not mostly

I am the construct of some unwinnable race
a DNA scar tissue
warning coloration*

a who we are, tongues out,
backs bent

service to predators

Candyman

After Kara Walker's African't

A pollination
dressed in bark
parades
into the show,
unwilling

retribution
salts the soil
sprouting gourds of
green lust
to tickle
a girl's nose
or bosom
once blossomed

a staining,
inhaling a sugared
song of your pain
creasing the hours
that are ours, alone
awake.

Upon the realization that I don't have a natural habitat

I worry mi gente will never see me if I don't speak Spanish   but why
demonize dad
                                 (the third fairest of
                     his brood of 13—NO, I'm not adopted)
                     for not teaching

why should he had   it's not his people's language   anyway. not
anymore than English is mine

                     23&Me can't make me pronounce an old world.

(I do speak some Irish, [Gaeilge in Standard *Irish*], sometimes known as *Irish
Gaelic*
) & when I use my mother's Connacht maiden name
there, whew…

                     negation ain't new

Goya ain't even Puerto Rican

I think I'd prefer the language of El Taíno   (if I pronounced
that correctly)

Las primeras estrellas brillantes that, some say,
spoke   on the
different   same
languages   island (!)

(After the men were killed & women's children re
                             named—maybe that is eating
                             your young? [That is some Goya
                             shit!]
            Los conquistadores en caballos marrones)

we don't speak the history of,

anyhoo I'm Black on Ohlone land,

tongues

we don't speak the history of,

I know why I'm hard to translate
Why it's harder to
imitate. Reproduce. Anyway

… me gustaría to pass on la historia

as a Latinx?*
      sin   having   · to restate   in the language
we can understand me, inside of,

*Latinxs are a people. Many peoples. They don't necessarily speak Latin. But somewhere along their vines, the ancestors were colonized by the Spanish (or Portuguese). We don't say Hispanic anymore but Hispania was a place. I don't like the word Hispanic but the term pre-Hispanic makes sense to me. The Roman Empire occupied many places & called it romance. There were babies. & then the young ate the old. There are many Romance languages, Spanish is one of them, but the people who speak them aren't all called Latino/a/x. I answer to many things. I can be romantic.

Benediction

Praise to the girls running the world with charcoal amulets, burnt spells of an old world—marbled gravities of will.

Praise to the cantinas spilling Cronopios onto the street. Where else would those poets learn the map of dispossessions, sing the collapse of stars?

Praise to the pigeons who loiter the extravagances of Dublin & Old San Juan. They buck & stitch strands of the madrigal, a loop & root.

Part III
Ireland

Presentiment

Don't throw stones at blackbirds,
because it might not be a blackbird at all.

—*Jamaica Kincaid*

Munster's winter reveals
stillborn untruths

in pillows of saline
pre-sun.

A hailstorm of ice roe &
unpromise
flouting in spawn

a satin breach of birds,
a book, a psalm.

By scabbed night
air is thinner, piercing,

as a parched escape
masks in trance.

I finally hear

I'm finally here &
understand the need for

amniotic drain
a wet brain…

by darkness,
declaration—

Don't be scared of ghosts
they have no business with you

grandmother whispers

all rout would happen

eyes on the living

by dry light of day.

The crow is barking up a storm

at Saint Fin Barre's
this morning.
It's about last night's row.

Men are violence!

*I can yell all night
sunrise is pointless,
the aim at dark,
distraction...*

& a day
is gone.

You brought the gulls!

Five black males talk,
they call it a murder.

*They act as though we
don't honor our dead.
They personify...*

A magpie out of frame,
just one, little blackbird watches,

mistaken for raven
gifted bread by
an American poet.

A huff, &
off the church pew
he chews
rye & shame.

Upon the realization that I don't have a natural habitat II

atop the pews
Black & shimmering

a public pyramid
a party of few

    Northern flickers
    follow me:

    All shadow play when
    you can be Rebellion

    anyway, this simulation
    will cost you.

FOURTEENTH CENSUS OF THE UNITED STATES: 1920—POPULATION

STATE North Carolina
COUNTY Robeson
TOWNSHIP OR OTHER DIVISION OF COUNTY Pine Grove
NAME OF INCORPORATED PLACE
SUPERVISOR'S DISTRICT NO. 311
ENUMERATION DISTRICT NO. 10
SHEET NO. 8
WARD OF CITY

ENUMERATED BY ME ON THE ___ DAY OF January, 1920. ___ ENUMERATOR

Name:	Pansy Brown
Age:	15
Estimated Birth Year:	abt 1925
Gender:	Female
Race:	Negro (Black)
Birthplace:	South Carolina
Marital Status:	Single
Relation to Head of House:	Daughter
Home in 1940:	Pine Grove, Calhoun, South Carolina
Map of Home in 1940:	Pine Grove, Calhoun, South Carolina
Inferred Residence in 1935:	Pine Grove, Calhoun, South Carolina
Residence in 1935:	Pine Grove
Sheet Number:	11A
Occupation:	Farm Laborer
Industry:	Farm
Attended School or College:	Yes
Highest Grade Completed:	Elementary school, 3rd grade
Class of Worker:	Unpaid family worker
Weeks Worked in 1939:	8
Income:	25
Income Other Sources:	No

Census information via Ancestry.com

An é Éireannach ata ionat?

With thanks to Ciara Ní É

...my family, like most black American families, has not one but several white ancestors – men who took advantage of their access to young enslaved women... 'Kiss Me, I'm Irish' took on a whole new meaning for me, when I discovered that I was.
—Michael W Twitty
The Guardian

My mother's maiden name
no O'

something about *souperism*
family tradition

one of ours
consumed

betrayal,
sustenance,

& he's ours,
he,

beyond a .com ancestry
aren't we

beyond pride
forcibly wrung out

under chains &
labor laundries

a stench
a shamed swelling

a breaching

a brined transaction

stained-heat
-red planks

blood-orange-
green streams of

belligerency
we too know

ivory-stroked
false purity—

of course, I've
the hunger in me

generations of premature
goodbyes, calamity.

Do you ever stop

& wonder what you too lost
Or nah, it's cool here

I don't need your help. I just need you to recognize that this shit is killing you,
too, however much more softly, you stupid motherfucker, you know?
— *Fred Hampton floating above* **Fred Moten**

Could this melody
Be sung in other countries
By other birds?

—Richard Wright

Selkie

An earthly nurse sits & sings
—the wailing waters below ***Joan Baez***

if i'd bred
my side of the water

speaking in tongues
for men I'd loved

& laid on jagged shell
i'd be chanting *almost*

absorbing ghosts &
living shadows

Last & Original of Her Species

He takes my numb in hand,
            blows.

       We are concurrent,

despite the thrashing Irish sea. I am
home yet I quiver, he is

commandeering waves,
&

       I am surprised

how buoyant my body can be.

He aims his head
at my core,
hums to our gorgeously mixed
 & imagined progeny.

He holds me
&

I light up under full moon, yearning for the
unplanned
     .   I am afloat,
yet no longer fertile or resolute

in the ways of the women he will
love on land. Inside his hands

I grow gills & scales
& hear warnings

       across the fog siloed Merrow
           sound alarm

of still estuaries
babies have gone

as our legacy
dissolves in song.

why do you flutter,
skimming oceans on damp wings
misnamed Desire?

Crane Lane, Last Call

Know which parts of him you want

his mouth
       a gin't tobacco tart

a fire familiar—
    an
ash awakening.

His eyes a makeshift
aperture

offering a scratched reel
of this moment

(you are bucket list
& parched)

& all the others

you wanted—

a bold flash
discreet smolder.

Birthday

        The late-May hue of impending June,
5am buzzed sleep
claws at 40$^+$ flames,

a frame of lashes between yesterday & hastening expiry.

Christmas Cakes you & the hold outs
called across the Pacific

 out of date.

It's funny
  how we all knead
     for celebration,

we lap the sun
& blow on honeycomb

bidding this isn't it,
all we get in smoke.

Drink Before the War

The bells of St. Fin Barre, off
five faint chimes & warring finches

2:41am birdsongs sculpt slim air
rollers, tits, a fidgeting pigeon

crashes—neck feathers bobbing,
weaving warning:

no one with roots doubled under
can survive these days

I tried   I've travelled   I'm tired

quickly decipher—thrasher, starling…
define invasive species, mimicry

can't tell if the cry is crow or my stomach
God protect me from its sensual coo.

In Cork, in a manner, to a degree, haunted means lucky. Luck can be defined as force, events, or circumstances that operate for or against an individual.

Meanwhile a circumstance could be evidence, cause, place, or a condition. It could also be life experience, the most indefinite argument anyone might try to live through.

The dawn to end all nights
That's all we hoped it was
A break from the warfare in your house
To each his own
A soldier is bailing out
& curled her lips on the barrel
& I don't know if the dead can talk
To anyone

—*Broken Bells*
The High Road

Legend

fire—(the West Coast of the US)
                                               /

untold lost   \

/   / scraping skin cross
country
     \   /
       —   **space** — —

what is found

(the Atlantic)—**water**
                  /

\
        in   /
\
rejourney

    /

\   /

\   a flooding
home
       /
air   \

~~scorched~~ **earth**—(Ireland)

Acknowledgements
(for early versions of these poems)

"Paradise as tinder" and "Candyman" appeared in *The Poetry Review* fall 2020

"Séance at the Beauty Parlor" appeared in *Obsidian: Literature & Arts in the African Diaspora* issue 49.1

"Ascension" appeared in *Hayden's Ferry Review* issue 71

"Upon the realization that you don't have a natural habitat" appeared in *Sporklet 2022*

"Pirouettes", "We're Going to Save Us" and "A hyphen is a rejection of negative space" appeared in the October 2020 *Works of Resistance, Resilience* issue of *About Place Journal*

"The Fever Dream" appeared in *WRITTEN HERE + THERE: The Community of Writers Poetry Review 2020*

"Rusty, this is a poem about Lexapro" appeared in *Newtown Literary* summer 2020

"Stain in Creases" appeared in *Poetry Ireland* spring 2021

"Presentiment" appeared in *Poetry London* fall 2022

"The crow is barking up a storm" appeared in *The Stinging Fly* summer 2020

"Literacy" and "Tim Burton says I'm not his aesthetic" appeared in *The Stinging Fly* summer 2022

"On the ghettoization of childless women" and "Last & Original of Her Species" appeared in *PROTOTYPE 4*

"Crane Lane, Last Call", "Birthday", "Drink Before the War" and "We are all drowned out" appeared on *Poethead* June 2020

"Sonnets" appeared in *Southword* fall 2021

"An é Éireannach ata ionat?" appeared in *Quarryman* spring 2020

Logistical Notes

"Manuscript Found in a Bottle. The colossal waters rear their heads above us like demons of the deep" or "The colossal waters rear our heads above us like demons of the deep," cover image by Harry Clarke, c. 1919 or 1923. This image is in the public domain.

'The Great Race Place' is a nickname for the racetrack in Santa Anita Park in Arcadia, California. It is one of the deadliest sites for animals that are forced to participate in the inhumane sport of horseracing. The horse stalls on the grounds also served as Internment sites or Wartime Civil Control Administration camps for Japanese Americans.

Samuel Little's FBI sketches via FBI.com on page 35 are in the public domain.

The image on page 47 is "There flashed upward a glow and a glare" by Harry Clarke, c. 1919. This image is in the public domain.

The image on page 91 is "Very Nearly" by Harry Clarke, c. 1920. This image is in the public domain.

A note on "On the ghettoization of childless women": This poem is not a dig at Maggie Smith or "Good Bones" as much as it's about my disdain for how the poem was appropriated on social media during a very difficult time for everyone, but especially for those of us who quarantined without partners or children.

Crane Lane is a catch all, end-of-night bar in Cork.

The image on page 100 is "The boat appeared to be hanging, as if by magic,... upon the interior surface of a funnel" by Harry Clarke, c. 1919. This image is in the public domain.

The best way to describe the ghost text in this book is to call them mystical parentheticals. They are the voices of those that have past, those that never had the chance to live, & those who are currently battling against their own disappearing.

The poetry films linked by QR codes in this book can also be found online:

https://www.youtube.com/watch?v=fHO33geg2wQ&t=4s
Presentiment

https://www.youtube.com/watch?v=BB4DF-0xA3E
The Crow is Barking Up A Storm

https://www.youtube.com/watch?v=XgiTes0yWH0
We Are All Drowned Out

Personal Notes

San Francisco was always my "you've made it" city, my dream home, so attempting to settle there to begrudgingly discover that my journey would not end there was heartbreaking… & a true beginning.

Thank you to Dr. Joy Viveros at San Francisco State University for helping me find my voice.

Thank you to Fulbright Ireland, The Arts Council of Ireland & University College Cork for the most amazing second wind.

Thank you to Cal Doyle, the mayor of Cork, so to speak. Thanks for taking me & my work seriously before anyone made that a thing to do.

I worked on most of this book during & through (?) the Black Spring (I don't even know what to call the era of tripping over black boxes left by the 'well-meaning & newly enlightened' on Instagram anymore) while attending the Tin House & Community of Writers poetry workshops, the Sewanee Writers' Conference, The Palm Beach Poetry Festival, a Hambidge residency, a CantoMundo retreat, & numerous Cave Canem workshops. Thank you to all of those organizations for offering me the scholarship, time & space to grow.

I have so many teachers to thank for their genius & attention during the writing of this book, including: Dr. Kwame Dawes, Eduardo C. Corral, Ladan Osman, Dr. Barry Monahan &, always, Camille Dungy.

Thank you to my UNL peeps (& soon-to-be-Drs!), especially Ian Maxton (a goddamn fiction writer!), for giving me that final push during Writing Center hours. & thanks to Dr. Rachel Azima for making the Writing Center at UNL what it is.

Thank you to Shanna Compton for helping to guide the design of this book. From copywriting at Macys to this, who'd have thunk it?

& always, thank you to my grandmother, Pansy Brown, for enduring this world.

Kimberly Reyes is an award-winning poet and essayist. Her work is featured in various international outlets including The Atlantic, The New York Times, The Associated Press, Entertainment Weekly, Time.com, The Village Voice, Alternative Press, ESPN the Magazine, Film Ireland, The Poetry Review, Poetry London, Poetry Ireland, The Irish Examiner, RTÉ Radio, NY1 News, The Best American Poetry blog, poets.org, American Poets Magazine, The Feminist Wire, and The Stinging Fly. Kimberly Reyes has received fellowships and residencies from the Poetry Foundation, the Academy of American Poets, the Fulbright Program, CantoMundo, Callaloo, Sewanee Writers' Conference, Tin House Workshops, the Arts Council of Ireland, Hambidge, Culture Ireland, the New York Foundation for the Arts, the Munster Literature Centre and many other places. Kimberly wrote this book while splitting her time between San Francisco, Ireland, and her hometown of New York City. She is currently a PhD student in Creative Writing-Poetry at the University of Nebraska—Lincoln.

vanishing point.
by Kimberly Reyes
Cover art by Harry Clarke

Cover design by Shanna Compton
Interior design by Kimberly Reyes and Laura Joakimson
Interior typeface: Times New Roman

Printed in the United States
by Books International, Dulles, Virginia

Publication of this book was made possible in part by gifts from
Katherine & John Gravendyk in honor of Hillary Gravendyk,
Francesca Bell, Mary Mackey, and The New Place Fund

Omnidawn Publishing
Oakland, California
Staff and Volunteers, Spring 2023
Rusty Morrison, senior editor & publisher
Laura Joakimson, executive director
Rob Hendricks, poetry & fiction, & post-pub marketing
Sharon Zetter, poetry editor & book designer
Jeffrey Kingman, copy editor
Liza Flum, poetry editor
Anthony Cody, poetry editor
Jason Bayani, poetry editor
Gail Aronson, fiction editor
Jennifer Metsker, marketing assistant
Sophia Carr, marketing assistant